Wheat-Free Classics

Lunch for Kids Recipes

All Rights Reserved. No part of this publication may be reproduced in any form or by any means, including scanning, photocopying, or otherwise without prior written permission of the copyright holder.
Copyright © 2013

Introduction

The health of our children is an active battle we must wage in a world of wheat-based foods, refined sugars, processed foods, harmful chemicals and the ever-present happy meal. Unfortunately, junk food is the most convenient food option that is often targeted at little ones. Getting kids vitamins and nutrients in their daily food takes the strategy of a military sergeant. Not to worry, this recipe book is here to help at one of the most vulnerable times. The school lunch. Unfortunately, many schools offer unhealthy foods that are not planned with the ultimate health benefits that kids need as their bodies are rapidly developing.

Try these healthy school lunch ideas for a variety of all-natural whole food combinations that kids will surprisingly love. Worried they won't go for the healthy foods? Keep these lunches out of school trash cans by using natural sweeteners provided by good old Mother Nature including raw honey, agave nectar, bananas and more. With obesity statistics on the rise and many other problems being linked to diet, it has never been more important to make sure kids are eating whole and helpful foods. Keep them strong, focused and healthy with these convenient lunch recipes.

Table of Contents

Cashew Butter And Banana Sandwich
Almond Butter and Strawberry Sandwich
Beef Bun
Cocoa Cream Bun
Honey Nut Bun
Chicken Pot Pie
Lamb Pot Pie
Meatballs
Bacon Baked Apples
Peach Pecan "Fried" Pie
Sweet Potato "Fried" Pie
Asian Empanada
Jamaican Jerk Patty
Chicken Tenders
Turkey Tenders
Pita Bites
Homemade Applesauce
Banana Pudding
Pizza Bites
Soft Baked Pretzel
Frontier Anzac Biscuits
Cream Filled Carrot Cake Muffin
Sausage Stuffed "Corn" Muffin

Baby BLT
Cheese Steak Sandwich

Cashew Butter And Banana Sandwich

Prep Time: 10 minutes

Cook Time: 20 minutes

Servings: 4

INGREDIENTS

Sandwich Bread

1 cup tapioca flour/starch

1/4 - 1/3 cup coconut flour

1 egg

1/2 cup warm water

1/4 cup coconut oil

1/4 cup applesauce

1 tablespoon sweetener*

1 teaspoon apple cider vinegar

1/2 teaspoon baking soda

1/2 teaspoon cinnamon

1/2 teaspoon sea salt

Filling

1/2 cup cashews (raw or roasted)

2 tablespoons coconut oil

1 tablespoon sweetener*

1/4 teaspoon cinnamon

1 banana

INSTRUCTIONS

1. Preheat oven to 350 degrees F. Line sheet pan with parchment paper or coat with coconut oil.
2. In medium bowl, sift together tapioca flour, 1/4 cup coconut flour, baking soda and salt. Stir in warm water and oil.
3. Whisk egg in small bowl. Add applesauce, vinegar and cinnamon. Add egg mixture to flour mixture and mix until well combined. Add 1 tablespoon coconut flour or water at a time if needed to form soft and slightly sticky dough.
4. Divide dough into 4 portions and roll into round or oval balls. Dust your hand with extra tapioca flour to prevent sticking.
5. Place rolls on sheet pan and pat down slightly. Bake 20 minutes, or until edges are golden brown and the tops are firm. Remove from oven and allow to cool.
6. While *Sandwich Bread* is baking, add cashews, coconut oil, sweetener and cinnamon to food processor or bullet blender and process until smooth. Add 1/2 tablespoon of coconut oil at a time if necessary to reach preferred consistency. Or use jarred cashew butter.
7. Slice bananas. Slice cooled *Sandwich Bread* in half and spread on cashew butter. Layer banana slices on bread.
8. Serve immediately. Or wrap in plastic wrap or parchment and store in lidded container.

stevia, raw honey or agave nectar

Almond Butter and Strawberry Sandwich

Prep Time: 10 minutes
Cook Time: 20 minutes
Servings: 4

INGREDIENTS

Sandwich Bread

1 cup tapioca flour/starch

1/4 - 1/3 cup coconut flour

1 egg

1/2 cup warm water

1/4 cup coconut oil

1/4 cup applesauce

1 tablespoon sweetener*

1 teaspoon apple cider vinegar

1/2 teaspoon cinnamon

1/4 teaspoon ground ginger

1/2 teaspoon baking soda

1/2 teaspoon sea salt

Filling

1/2 cup almonds (raw or roasted)

2 tablespoons coconut oil

1 tablespoon sweetener*

1/4 teaspoon cinnamon

1/4 teaspoon ground ginger

5 - 6 medium strawberries

INSTRUCTIONS

1. Preheat oven to 350 degrees F. Line sheet pan with parchment paper or coat with coconut oil.
2. In medium bowl, sift together tapioca flour, 1/4 cup coconut flour, baking soda and salt. Stir in warm water and oil.
3. Whisk egg in small bowl. Add applesauce, vinegar, cinnamon and ginger. Add egg mixture to flour mixture and mix until well combined. Add 1 tablespoon coconut flour or water at a time if needed to form soft and slightly sticky dough.
4. Divide dough into 4 portions and roll into round or oval balls. Dust your hand with extra tapioca flour to prevent sticking.
5. Place rolls on sheet pan and pat down slightly. Bake 20 minutes, or until edges are golden brown and the tops are firm. Remove from oven and allow to cool.
6. While *Sandwich Bread* is baking, add almonds, coconut oil, sweetener, cinnamon and ginger to food processor or bullet blender and process until smooth. Add 1/2 tablespoon of coconut oil at a time if necessary to reach preferred consistency. Or use jarred almond butter.
7. Slice strawberries. Slice cooled *Sandwich Bread* in half and spread on almond butter. Layer strawberry slices on bread.
8. Serve immediately. Or wrap in plastic wrap or parchment and store in lidded container.

stevia, raw honey or agave nectar

Beef Bun

Prep Time: 15 minutes

Cook Time: 30 minutes

Servings: 4

INGREDIENTS

Bun

1 cup tapioca flour/starch

1/4 - 1/3 cup coconut flour

1 egg

1/2 cup warm water

1/2 cup coconut oil

1 teaspoon apple cider vinegar

1/2 teaspoon baking soda

1 teaspoon sea salt

Filling

8 ozground beef

1/2 small onion

1 garlic clove

1 teaspoon ground cumin

1/2 teaspoon chili powder

1/4 teaspoon cayenne

1/2 teaspoon ground black pepper

1/2 teaspoon Sea salt

INSTRUCTIONS

1. Preheat oven to 350 degrees F. Line sheet pan with parchment paper or coat with coconut oil. Heat medium skillet over medium-high heat.
2. For *Filling*, grind or mince onion and add to skillet with beef, salt and spices. Sauté until cooked through and browned, about 8 - 10 minutes. Remove from heat and set aside.
3. In medium bowl, sift together tapioca flour, 1/4 cup coconut flour, baking soda and salt. Stir in warm water and oil.
4. Whisk egg and vinegar in small bowl. Add egg mixture to flour mixture and mix until well combined. Add 1 tablespoon coconut flour or water at a time if needed to form soft and slightly sticky dough.
5. Divide dough into 4 portions and flatten into round disks. Dust your hand or rolling pin with extra tapioca flour to prevent sticking.
6. Scoop beef filling into center of dough disks and pinch edged of dough together to create round, sealed ball.
7. Place buns sealed side down on sheet pan and pat down slightly. Bake 20 minutes, or until edges are golden brown and dough is cooked through.
8. Serve immediately. Or store in lidded container.

Cocoa Cream Bun

Prep Time: 10 minutes

Cook Time: 20 minutes

Servings: 4

INGREDIENTS

Bun

1 cup tapioca flour/starch

1/4 - 1/3 cup coconut flour

1 egg

1/2 cup warm water

1/2 cup coconut oil

1 tablespoon sweetener*

1 teaspoon apple cider vinegar

1 tablespoon cocoa powder

1/2 teaspoon cinnamon

1/2 teaspoon baking soda

1/2 teaspoon sea salt

Filling

1 cup cashews (raw or roasted)

2 tablespoons coconut cream

2 tablespoons coconut oil

2 tablespoons cocoa powder

3 tablespoons sweetener*

1/2 teaspoon cinnamon

INSTRUCTIONS

1. Preheat oven to 350 degrees F. Line sheet pan with parchment paper or coat with coconut oil. Heat medium skillet over medium-high heat.
2. For *Filling*, add cashews, coconut oil, coconut cream, cocoa powder, sweetener and cinnamon to food processor or bullet blender and process until smooth. Add 1/2 tablespoon coconut oil at a time if needed to reach desired consistency. Set aside.
3. In medium bowl, sift together tapioca flour, 1/4 cup coconut flour, cocoa powder, cinnamon, baking soda and salt. Stir in warm water and oil.
4. Whisk egg in small mixing bowl. Add sweetenerand vinegar. Add egg mixture to flour mixture and mix until well combined. Add 1 tablespoon coconut flour or water at a time if needed to form soft and slightly sticky dough.
5. Divide dough into 4 portions and flatten into round disks. Dust your hand or rolling pin with extra tapioca flour to prevent sticking.
6. Scoop *Filling* into center of dough disks and pinch edges of dough together to create round, sealed ball.
7. Place buns sealed side down on sheet pan and pat down slightly. Bake 20 minutes, or until edges are golden brown and dough is cooked through.
8. Serve immediately. Or store in lidded container.

stevia, raw honey or agave nectar

Honey Nut Bun

Prep Time: 15 minutes

Cook Time: 30 minutes

Servings: 4

INGREDIENTS

Bun

1 cup tapioca flour/starch

1/4 - 1/3 cup coconut flour

1 egg

1/2 cup warm water

1/2 cup coconut oil

1 teaspoon apple cider vinegar

1 teaspoon vanilla

1/2 teaspoon cinnamon

1/2 teaspoon baking soda

1/2 teaspoon sea salt

Filling

1 cup walnuts

1/4 cup sweetener*

2 teaspoons cinnamon

1 teaspoon ground ginger

INSTRUCTIONS

1. Preheat oven to 350 degrees F. Line sheet pan with parchment paper or coat with coconut oil. Heat medium skillet over medium-high heat.
2. For *Filling*, mix walnuts, sweetener, cinnamon and ginger in small mixing bowl. Set aside.
3. In medium bowl, sift together tapioca flour, 1/4 cup coconut flour, vanilla, cinnamon, baking soda and salt. Stir in warm water and oil.
4. Whisk egg and vinegar in small bowl. Add egg mixture to flour mixture and mix until well combined.
5. Add 1 tablespoon coconut flour or water at a time if needed to form soft and slightly sticky dough.
6. Divide dough into 4 portions and flatten into round disks. Dust your hand or rolling pin with extra tapioca flour to prevent sticking.
7. Scoop *Filling* into center of dough disks and pinch edges of dough together to create round, sealed ball.
8. Place buns sealed side down on sheet pan and pat down slightly. Bake 20 minutes, or until edges are golden brown and dough is cooked through.
9. Serve immediately. Or store in lidded container.

stevia, raw honey or agave nectar

Chicken Pot Pie

Prep Time: 15 minutes

Cook Time: 30 minutes

Servings: 4

INGREDIENTS

Filling

8 ozskin-on chicken

1 1/2 cup chicken broth

2 tablespoons tapioca flour

2 tablespoons coconut oil

2 carrots

1 celery stalk

1 green bell pepper

1 small onion

2 garlic cloves

2 teaspoons dried thyme (or 4 teaspoons fresh thyme)

1 tablespoon lemon juice

1/2 teaspoon black pepper

Pinch sea salt

Crust

1/3 cup almond flour

2 tablespoons coconut flour

3 tablespoons cold coconut oil (or cacao butter)

1 egg

3 - 4 teaspoons water

1/2 teaspoon dried thyme

1/4 teaspoon sea salt

INSTRUCTIONS

1. Preheat oven to 400 degrees F. Heat medium pot over medium heat.
2. Add two tablespoon coconut oil to hot pot. Add chicken pieces skin side down. Cook about 3 minutes, then turn with tongs and continue cooking another 3 minutes. Remove chicken and set aside.
3. Whisk coconut flourinto pot until smooth. Gradually whisk in chicken broth.Simmer about 5 minutes, whisking occasionally.
4. Peel and mince garlic. Chop carrots, celery, onion and bell pepper. Add to pot with thyme, salt pepper and lemon juice.
5. Chop par-cooked chicken meat. Add back to pot and simmer for 5 minutes. Remove from heat and set aside.
6. For *Crust*, add cold coconut oil to flours, thyme and salt in small bowl. Cut fat into flour with fork until crumbly. Mix in egg and enough water to bring together tender dough.
7. Divide dough into 4 portions. Roll into balls and flatten into round disks large enough to fit over mini pie tins or ceramic ramekins with hand, then rolling pin.
8. Pour *Filling* intovessels and cover with crusts. Pinch edges of dough over edges of vessels to seal in liquid. Brush top of each pie with coconut oil, coconut milk, or egg wash and sprinkle with salt. Use knife to cut a slit in the top of each pie.
9. Bake pot pies for about 15 minutes, until crust is golden.
10. Remove from oven and allow pies to cool for 10 minutes.

11. Serve warm. Or let cool completely and serve room temperature.

Lamb Pot Pie

Prep Time: 15 minutes

Cook Time: 30 minutes

Servings: 4

INGREDIENTS

Filling

8 oz lamb

1 1/2 cup beef or vegetable broth

2 tablespoons tapioca flour

2 tablespoons coconut oil

2 chopped carrots

1 chopped celery stalk

1 bell pepper (yellow, orange or red)

1 small green tomato (or under ripe red tomato)

1 small onion

2 garlic cloves

1 inch piece ginger

1 tablespoon curry powder

1 tablespoon ground coriander

1 teaspoon ground cumin

1/2 teaspoon ground cinnamon

1/2 teaspoon black pepper

Pinch sea salt

Crust

1/3 cup almond flour

2 tablespoons coconut flour

3 tablespoons cold coconut oil (or cacao butter)

1 egg

3 - 4 teaspoons water

1/2 teaspoon turmeric

1/4 teaspoon sea salt

INSTRUCTIONS
1. Preheat oven to 400 degrees F. Heat medium pot over medium heat.
2. Add two tablespoon coconut oil to hot pot. Add lamb. Sauté about 5 minutes, then remove lamb with tongs.
3. Whisk in coconut flour until smooth. Gradually whisk in broth. Simmer about 5 minutes, whisking occasionally.
4. Peel and mince garlic and ginger. Chop carrots, celery, onion, bell pepper and tomato. Add to pot with salt, and spices.
5. Chop par-cooked lamb meat. Add lamb back to pot and simmer for 5 minutes. Remove from heat and set aside.
6. For *Crust*, add cold coconut oil to flours, turmeric and salt in small bowl. Cut fat into flour with fork until crumbly. Mix in egg and enough water to bring together tender dough.
7. Divide dough into 4 portions. Roll into balls and flatten into round disks large enough to fit over mini pie tins or ceramic ramekins with hand, then rolling pin.
8. Pour *Filling* into vessels and cover with crusts. Pinch edges of dough over edges of vessels to seal in liquid. Brush top of each pie with coconut oil, coconut milk, or egg wash and sprinkle with salt. Use knife to cut a slit in the top of each pie.

9. Bake pot pies for about 15 minutes, until crust is golden.
10. Remove from oven and allow pies to cool for 10 minutes.
11. Serve warm. Or let cool completely and serve room temperature.

Meatballs

Prep Time: 5 minutes

Cook Time: 20 minutes

Servings: 4

INGREDIENTS

16 oz (1 lb) ground meat (beef, pork, chicken, bison, or any combination)

1 cup almond flour

1 egg

1 garlic clove

1/2 small onion

1 teaspoon dried parsley

1 teaspoon dried oregano

1/2 teaspoon ground black pepper

1/2 teaspoon sea salt

Tomato Sauce

4 oz organic tomato sauce

4 oz organic crushed tomatoes

1 teaspoon dried oregano

1/2 teaspoon dried basil

1/2 teaspoon ground black pepper

DIRECTIONS

1. Preheat oven to 350 degrees. Line baking sheet with parchment or baking mat. Or prepare glass or ceramic casserole dish.

2. Pulse onion and garlic in food processor or blender until finely processed, but before paste forms. Or finely mince onion and garlic.
3. Beat egg in large bowl. Add ground meat, almond flour, spices and salt. Mix well with hands or large wooden spoon.
4. Form 18 - 24 meatballs with scoop or tablespoon, then roll in hands.
5. Arrange meatballs on lines sheet pan or in casserole dish and bake for 15 to 20 minutes, until golden brown and cooked through.
6. Add all *Tomato Sauce* ingredients to small pot and heat over medium heat. Stir and simmer about 10 minutes, until reduced and thickened.
7. Remove meatballs from oven. Toss with *Tomato Sauce* and serve hot.
8. Or allow meatballs and *Tomato Sauce* to cool, then pack in lidded containers. Serve room temperature.

Bacon Baked Apples

Prep Time: 15 minutes

Cook Time: 30 minutes

Servings: 4

INGREDIENTS

6 oz nitrate-free bacon (thick slices or whole slab)

4 tart apples

4 dried apricots

2 tablespoons dried cranberries

2 tablespoons dried cherries

2 tablespoons dried raisins

1 tablespoon cinnamon

Juice of half a lemon

Zest of half a lemon

Water

INSTRUCTIONS

1. Preheat oven to 350 degrees F. Heat medium skillet over medium-high heat.
2. Chop apricots. Add dried fruit to small bowl with lemon juice. Add enough water just to cover fruit. Let fruit rehydrate for 10 minutes.
3. Dice bacon and add to hot skillet. Sauté about 5 - 8 minutes, until crisp and golden brown.
4. Slice apples in half lengthwise. Carefully core apples, scooping out seeds, stem and tough core with melon baller. Leave good-sized well in apple.

5. Arrange apples in baking dish just large enough to fit them snuggly. Pour water into bottom of baking dish, about 1/8 inch.
6. Strain fruit, reserving liquid in small bowl. Strain bacon, reserving liquid. Mix lemon zest, cinnamon and bacon with fruit.
7. Fill apple wells with fruit mixture. Press down into apple, packing slightly.
8. Pour 1teaspoonreserved liquid and over each apple. Follow by 1 tablespoon bacon grease over all 8 apple halves.
9. Bake in preheated oven for 20-30 minutes, until apples are tender.
10. Serve warm. Or allow to cooled completely, and store in lidded container.

Peach Pecan "Fried" Pie

Prep Time: 20 minutes

Cook Time: 20 minutes

Servings: 4

INSTRUCTIONS

Crust

2 cups almond flour

2 eggs

3 tablespoons coconut oil

1 tablespoon sweetener*

1/4 teaspoon baking soda

1 teaspoon ground cinnamon

1/2 teaspoon sea salt

Filling

2 peaches

1/4 cup dried apricots

1/4 cup pecans

2 tablespoons sweetener*

2 tablespoons water

1 tablespoon ground cinnamon

1 teaspoon vanilla

1/2 teaspoon ground ginger

DIRECTIONS

1. Preheat oven to 400 degrees. Line sheet pan with parchment or baking mat. Cover cutting board with parchment.
2. For *Crust*, sift almond flour into medium mixing bowl. Add baking soda, cinnamon and salt.
3. Whisk eggs and sweetener in small mixing bowl, then add to flour and combine. Slowly add coconut oil until malleable dough comes together.
4. Roll in plastic wrap or wrap tightly in parchment and refrigerate for 15 minutes.
5. Heat medium pan over medium heat.
6. Peel and pit peaches. Chop apricots, pecans and peaches. Add to hot pan with sweetener, spices and water. Sauté about 5 - 10 minutes, until peaches are tender and
7. Remove dough from refrigerator. Roll dough out on parchment covered cutting board to about 1/8 inch thick square with rolling pin. Use sharp knife or pizza cutter to cut dough into 4 squares.
8. Scoop equal portions of *Filling* into center of one side of each dough square. Fold bare half of dough over filled half. Press edges together, letting any trapped air escape. Crimp edges of dough together with fork. Repeat with remaining dough.
9. Arrange pies on lined sheet pan and bake 15 - 20 minutes, or until dough is golden and cooked through.
10. Serve immediately. Or allow to cool and store in air-tight container.

stevia, raw honey or agave nectar

NOTE: Heat large skillet over medium heat, add 1/4 inch coconut oil, and fry pies 2 minutes on each side for traditional *Fried Pies*.

Sweet Potato "Fried" Pie

Prep Time: 20 minutes

Cook Time: 30 minutes

Servings: 4

INSTRUCTIONS

Crust

2 cups almond flour

2 eggs

3 tablespoons coconut oil

1 tablespoon sweetener*

1/4 teaspoon baking soda

1/2 teaspoon ground cinnamon

1/2 teaspoon sea salt

Filling

1 large sweet potato

1/2 cup dried dates

1/4 cup walnuts

1 egg

1 teaspoon vanilla

1 teaspoon ground cinnamon

1 teaspoon ground nutmeg

1/2 teaspoon ground black pepper

DIRECTIONS

1. Bring medium pot of lightly salted water to boil. Cover cutting board with parchment.
2. For *Crust*, sift almond flour into medium mixing bowl. Add baking soda, cinnamon and salt.
3. Whisk eggs and sweetener in small mixing bowl, then add to flour and combine. Slowly add coconut oil until malleable dough comes together.
4. Roll in plastic wrap or wrap tightly in parchment and refrigerate for 15 minutes.
5. Preheat oven to 400 degrees. Line sheet pan with parchment or baking mat.
6. Peel and dice sweet potato. Chop dates. Add sweet potato and dates to boiling water peaches. Cook about 10 minutes, until sweet potatoes are soft. Drain sweet potatoes and dates.
7. Add egg to medium mixing bowl. Add 1 tablespoon hot sweet potatoes to bowl. Mash briefly, then add second tablespoon. Gradually add all hot sweet potatoes and dates to egg. Mash and mix, careful not to scramble egg. Stir in vanilla, cinnamon, nutmeg and pepper.
8. Chop walnuts. Set aside.
9. Remove dough from refrigerator. Roll dough out on parchment covered cutting board to about 1/8 inch thick square with rolling pin. Use sharp knife or pizza cutter to cut dough into 4 squares.
10. Scoop equal portions of *Filling* into center of one side of each dough square. Fold bare half of dough over filled half. Press edges together, letting any trapped air escape. Crimp edges of dough together with fork. Repeat with remaining dough.

11. Arrange pies on lined sheet pan and bake 15 - 20 minutes, or until dough is golden and cooked through.
12. Serve immediately. Or allow to cool and store in air-tight container.

stevia, raw honey or agave nectar

NOTE: Heat large skillet over medium heat , add 1/4 inch coconut oil, and fry pies 2 minutes on each side for traditional *Fried Pies*.

Asian Empanada

Prep Time: 20 minutes

Cook Time: 20 minutes

Servings: 4

INSTRUCTIONS

Crust

1 cup almond flour

1 cup coconut flour

2 eggs

3 tablespoons sesame oil (or coconut oil)

1/2 teaspoon garlic powder

1/2 teaspoon onion powder

1/2 teaspoon ground ginger

1/4 teaspoon baking soda

1 teaspoon sea salt

1 tablespoon sesame oil (or coconut oil)

1 tablespoon sesame seeds

Filling

6 oz chicken or shrimp

1/2 head cabbage (1 cup shredded)

1 carrot

1/4 cup mushrooms

2 inch piece fresh ginger

2 garlic cloves

1 tablespoon pure fish sauce

1 teaspoon apple cider vinegar

1 shallot

1 scallion

1 teaspoon sesame oil

DIRECTIONS

1. For *Crust*, sift almond and coconut flour into medium mixing bowl. Add baking soda, spices and salt.
2. Whisk eggs in small mixing bowl, then add to flour and combine. Slowly add 3 tablespoons oil until malleable dough comes together.
3. Roll in plastic wrap or wrap tightly in parchment and refrigerate for 15 minutes.
4. Preheat oven to 400 degrees. Line sheet pan with parchment or baking mat. Cover cutting board with parchment. Het medium pan over medium heat.
5. Shred cabbage, grate carrot, slice mushrooms. Peel and grate ginger. Slice scallion. Peel and mince shallot and garlic. Dice chicken or slice shrimp in half.
6. Add sesame oil to pan. Add chicken or shrimp hot oiled pan with ginger, shallot and garlic. Sauté about 90 seconds. Add cabbage, carrot, and mushrooms and sauté for a minute.
7. Add vinegar and fish sauce. Sauté about 3minutes until cabbage is wilted. Stir in scallions. Remove from heat and set aside.
8. Remove dough from refrigerator. Divide dough into 4 portions. Roll dough into balls and flatten on parchment covered cutting

board with hands. Roll into circles about 1/8 inch thick with rolling pin.
9. Scoop equal portions of *Filling* into center of one side of dough circle. Fold bare half of dough over filled half. Press edges together, letting any trapped air escape. Crimp edges of dough together with fork. Repeat with remaining dough.
10. Bruch tops of empanada with sesame oil and sprinkle with sesame seeds.
11. Arrange empanadas on lined sheet pan and bake 15 - 20 minutes, or until dough is golden and cooked through.
12. Serve immediately. Or allow to cool and store in air-tight container.

Jamaican Jerk Patty

Prep Time: 20 minutes

Cook Time: 30 minutes

Servings: 4

INSTRUCTIONS

Crust

2 cups almond flour

2 eggs

3 tablespoons coconut oil

1 teaspoon curry powder

1/4 teaspoon baking soda

1/2 teaspoon sea salt

Filling

8 ozmeat (ground or shredded chicken, beef or pork)

1 small onion

1 tablespoon curry powder

1 teaspoon allspice

1 teaspoon chile powder

1 teaspoon cayenne pepper

1 teaspoon red pepper flake

1/2 teaspoon garlic powder

1/2 teaspoon onion powder

1/2 teaspoon ground cinnamon

DIRECTIONS

1. For *Crust*, sift almond flour into medium mixing bowl. Add baking soda, curry powder and salt.
2. Whisk eggs in small mixing bowl, then add to flour and combine. Slowly add coconut oil until malleable dough comes together.
3. Roll in plastic wrap or wrap tightly in parchment and refrigerate for 15 minutes.
4. Preheat oven to 400 degrees. Line sheet pan with parchment or baking mat. Cover cutting board with parchment. Heat medium pan over medium heat.
5. Peel and mince onion. Add to hot pan with ground or shredded meat and spices. Sauté about 5 - 10 minutes, until beef is browned. Remove from heat and set aside.
6. Remove dough from refrigerator. Divide dough into 4 portions. Roll dough into balls and flatten on parchment covered cutting board with hands. Roll into circles about 1/8 inch thick with rolling pin.
7. Scoop equal portions of *Filling* into center of one side of dough circle. Fold bare half of dough over filled half. Press edges together, letting any trapped air escape. Crimp edges of dough together with fork. Repeat with remaining dough.
8. Arrange patties on lined sheet pan and bake 15 - 20 minutes, or until dough is golden and cooked through.
9. Serve immediately. Or allow to cool and store in air-tight container.

Chicken Tenders

Prep Time: 5 minutes

Cook Time: 10 minutes

Servings: 2

INGREDIENTS

8 oz boneless, skinless chicken

1 egg

1/2 cup almond meal

1 teaspoon flax meal

1 teaspoon paprika

1/2 teaspoon thyme

1/2 teaspoon onion powder

1/2 teaspoon ground black pepper

1/2 teaspoon sea salt

Honey Mustard

2 tablespoon raw honey or agave nectar

3 tablespoons organic mustard

INSTRUCTIONS

1. Heat a medium skillet over medium high heat. Lightly coat pan with coconut oil.
2. Slice chicken into 1 inch wide strips. Arrange slices between 2 sheets of parchment and pound with kitchen mallet or rolling pin to flatten slightly. Place flattened pieces between two paper towels to absorb excess moisture.

3. In a shallow dish, blend almond meal, flax meal, spices and salt.
4. Beat egg in small mixing bowl. Dip chicken into beaten egg, then dredge in seasoned almond meal.
5. Carefully place coated chicken strips into hot oil and fry about 3 - 4minutes, until golden brown and cooked through. Turn with tongs half way through cooking.
6. Drain cooked chicken on paper towel, then transfer to serving dish. Serve warm.
7. Or allow to cool and transfer to lidded container. Serve room temperature or chilled.
8. Mix mustard and sweetener in small serving bowl or lidded container. Serve with chicken.

stevia, raw honey or agave nectar

Turkey Tenders

Prep Time: 5 minutes

Cook Time: 15 minutes

Servings: 2

INGREDIENTS

8 oz boneless skinless turkey

1 egg

1/2 cup almond meal

1 teaspoon flax meal

1/4 teaspoon garlic powder

1/2 teaspoon paprika

1/2 teaspoon ground sage

1/2 teaspoon ground black pepper

1/2 teaspoon sea salt

Cranberry Compote

1/4 cup dried cranberries

1 teaspoon sweetener*

1/2 teaspoon arrowroot powder (or tapioca flour)

1/2 cup water

INSTRUCTIONS

1. Heat a medium skillet over medium high heat. Lightly coat pan with coconut oil. Heat small pot over medium heat. Add 1/2 cup water and bring to boil.

2. Slice turkey into 1 inch wide strips. Arrange slices between 2 sheets of parchment and pound with kitchen mallet or rolling pin to flatten slightly. Place turkey between two paper towels to absorb excess moisture.
3. Blend almond meal, flax meal, spices and salt in a shallow dish.
4. Beat egg in small mixing bowl. Dip turkey strips into beaten egg, then dredge in seasoned almond meal.
5. Carefully place coated turkey into hot oil and fry about 3 - 4 minutes, until golden brown and cooked through. Turn half way through cooking with tongs.
6. Add cranberries to boiling water, and whisk in sweetener and arrowroot or tapioca. Reduce heat to medium and stir occasionally as compote thickens, about 5 - 8 minutes.
7. Drain cooked turkey on paper towel, then transfer to serving dish. Serve warm.
8. Or allow to cool and transfer to lidded container. Serve room temperature or chilled.
9. Pour *Cranberry Compote* into small serving bowl or lidded container. Serve with chicken.

stevia, raw honey or agave nectar

Pita Bites

Prep Time: *5 minutes

Cook Time: 20 minutes

Servings: 1

INGREDIENTS

Pita Bites

1 cup tapioca flour/starch

1 teaspoon ground chia seed (or flax meal)

1 egg

2 tablespoons coconut oil

1/4 cup water

1/2 teaspoon baking soda

1/4 teaspoon sea salt

Almond Hummus

1 cup skinless almonds

1/3 cup tahini

1 garlic clove

Juice of 1/2 lemon

Zest of 1/2 lemon

1/4 teaspoon sea salt

1/4 cup water

2 tablespoons pine nuts

INSTRUCTIONS

1. *Soak almonds overnight in enough water to cover. Drain and rinse.
2. Preheat oven to 375 degrees F. Cover sheet pan with parchment paper or baking mat. Heat small pot over low heat.
3. For *Pita Bites*, mix 1/3 cup tapioca flour with chia meal, water and 1 tablespoon coconut oil in pot. Stir until mixture comes together. Remove from heat and cool in freezer.
4. In medium bowl, blend remaining tapioca flour, baking soda and salt. Then add egg and remaining oil. Mix until combined.
5. Add cooled chia mixture to bowl and mix to combine. Then remove and knead to form dough.
6. Form large round disk, then use rolling pin to flatten on lined baking sheet. Cut out circles with biscuit cutter or drinking glass, or cut triangles with pizza cutter. Re-roll excess dough and repeat until all dough is used.
7. Arrange pita pieces on sheet pan and place in oven. Bake about 10 minutes. Carefully turn over with spatula and bake another 5 - 7 minutes, or until crisp.
8. Remove from oven and let cool completely. Place in lidded container or sealable lunch bag and serve room temperature.
9. For *Almond Hummus*, add 1/2 of water to all ingredients in food processor or bullet blender and process. Add just enough water to smooth blend.
10. Scrape hummus into lidded container and serve chilled or room temperature with *Pita Bites*.

Homemade Applesauce

Prep Time: 10 minutes

Cook Time: 20 minutes

Servings: 4

INGREDIENTS

2 sweet apples

2 tart apples

1/4 cup sweetener*

3/4 cup water

1/2 teaspoon ground cinnamon

1/4 teaspoon ground ginger

INSTRUCTIONS

1. Peel, core and chop apples. Add to medium pan with sweetener, water and spices. Stir to combine.
2. Cover pan with lid, and heat pan over medium heat. Cook apples about 20 minutes. Transfer to heat-safe bowl and let cool about 5 minutes.
3. Mash apples with fork or potato masher. Then chill in refrigerator.
4. Transfer chilled applesauce to lidded container Serve chilled or room temperature.

Banana Pudding

Prep Time: 5 minutes

Cook Time: 15 minutes

Servings: 4

INGREDIENTS

3 overripe bananas

13 oz (1 can) full-fat coconut milk

2 egg yolks

1 tablespoon coconut oil

1 tablespoon almond butter (or cashew butter)

1 teaspoon vanilla

1 teaspoon ground cinnamon

INSTRUCTIONS

1. Heat medium pan over medium heat. Heat small pot over medium heat.
2. Add coconut milk, egg yolks and vanilla to pot and whisk until mixture starts to thicken. Remove from heat.
3. Add coconut oil and nut butter to pan. Add bananas and cinnamon, mashing a bit. Allow bananas to cook and caramelize slightly.
4. Pour thickened coconut milk mixture into food processor or blender. Add banana mixture and process until smooth.
5. Pour creamy pudding into serving bowls or lidded containers. To prevent skin from forming, lay sheet of plastic wrap directly over surface of serving bowls. Or secure lids on containers.
6. Refrigerate about 1 hour. Serve chilled.

Pizza Bites

Prep Time: 20 minutes*

Cook Time: 20 minutes

Servings: 4

INSTRUCTIONS

Crust

2 cups almond flour

2 eggs

3 tablespoons coconut oil

1/4 teaspoon baking soda

1 teaspoon sea salt

Almond Cheese

1 cup skinless almonds*

1/4 cup water

2 tablespoons coconut oil

1 tablespoon lemon juice

1 tablespoon apple cider vinegar

1 garlic clove

1/2 teaspoon sea salt

1/4 teaspoon ground white pepper (or black pepper)

Pizza Sauce

4 oz organic tomato paste

4 oz organic tomato sauce

1 teaspoon dried oregano

1/2 teaspoon dried basil

1/2 teaspoon ground black pepper

Filling

4 oz natural pepperoni

4 oz natural ground sausage

1/2 bell pepper

DIRECTIONS

1. *For *Almond Cheese*, soak almonds in 1 1/2 cups water overnight. Drain and rinse.
2. For *Crust*, sift almond flour into medium mixing bowl. Add baking soda, spices and salt.
3. Whisk eggs in small mixing bowl, then add to flour and combine. Slowly add coconut oil until malleable dough comes together.
4. Roll in plastic wrap or wrap tightly in parchment and refrigerate for 15 minutes.
5. Preheat oven to 400 degrees. Line sheet pan with parchment or baking mat. Cover cutting board with parchment. Heat medium pan over medium heat.
6. Seed and stem bell pepper. Dice pepper and pepperoni. Add peppers and sausage to hot pan. Sauté about 5 minutes, until sausage is cooked through. Transfer to small bowl to cool, and add diced pepperoni. Set aside.
7. Add all *Almond Cheese* ingredients to food processor or bullet blender and process until smooth. Add a few extra tablespoons of water if necessary to achieve thick but smooth consistency. Set aside.

8. In small bowl, mix together all *PizzaSauce* ingredients. Set aside.
9. Remove dough from refrigerator. Roll dough out on parchment covered cutting board with rolling pin to about 1/8 inch thickness. Use sharp knife or pizza cutter to cut dough into 2x4 inch rectangles.
10. Spread *Almond Cheese* in center of one half of each dough piece. Then dollop with small amount of *Pizza Sauce*, and a pinch of *Filling*.
11. Fold over bare half of dough. Press edges together, pressing out any trapped air. Use fork to crimp edges for better seal. Repeat with remaining dough.
12. Arrange *Pizza Bites* on lined sheet pan and bake 15 - 20 minutes, or until dough is golden and cooked through.
13. Serve immediately. Or allow to cool and store in air-tight container.

Soft Baked Pretzel

Prep Time: 15 minutes

Cook Time: 20 minutes

Servings: 4

INGREDIENTS

1 cup coconut flour

1/2 cup tapioca flour/starch

1/2 cup coconut oil

1/2 cup water

1 egg

2 tablespoon apple cider vinegar

1/2 teaspoon baking soda

1/2 teaspoon baking powder

1/2 teaspoon sea salt

INSTRUCTIONS

1. Preheat oven to 350 degrees F. Heat medium pan over medium-high heat. Line sheet pan with parchment or baking mat.
2. Add coconut oil, water, vinegar and salt to pot. Bring to a boil and remove from heat.
3. Whisk in tapioca flour. Stir with wooden spoon or soft spatula until mixture gels and comes together.
4. Stir in baking soda and baking powder. Continue mixing for a minute. Mixture will foam and expand. Let mixture sit and cool about 5 minutes.

5. Sift in coconut flour. Mix partially, then beat in egg. Blend until combined. Excess coconut flour may sit in bottom of bowl.
6. Turn out dough onto cutting board dusted with any excess coconut flour from mixture. Knead dough for 2 minutes.
7. Cut dough into 4 equal portions. Roll out pieces into ropes and twist to form classic pretzel twist. Pinch together any crumbled dough.
8. Arrange pretzels on lined sheet pan. Brush with coconut oil or full-fat coconut milk and sprinkle with salt.
9. Place sheet pan in oven and bake about 25 minutes, until cooked through.
10. Serve immediately with organic mustard. Or allow to cool and serve room temperature.

Frontier Anzac Biscuits

Prep Time: 5 minutes

Cook Time: 25 minutes

Servings: 4

INGREDIENTS

3/4 cup almond flour

3/4 cup sliced almonds

3/4 cup coconut flakes

1/4 cup sweetener*

1/4 cup coconut oil

1/2 teaspoon baking soda

1 tablespoon water

INSTRUCTIONS

1. Preheat oven to 300 degrees F. Line sheet pan with parchment sheet or baking mat.
2. In medium mixing bowl, combine almond flour, sliced almonds and coconut flakes.
3. Mix baking soda and water in small mixing bowl. Add to medium mixing bowl with sweetener and oil. Mix until combined. Add water 1 tablespoon at a time if dough is too crumbly.
4. Form 12 large biscuits and arrange on sheet pan. Flatten slightly with hand for even baking.
5. Bake for 25 - 30 minutes, until golden.
6. Serve immediately. Or allow to cool completely and pack in airtight container or sealable baggie.

* raw honey or agave nectar

Cream Filled Carrot Cake Muffin

Prep Time: 10 minutes*

Cook Time: 20 minutes

Servings: 12

INGREDIENTS

1 1/2 cups almond flour

2 tablespoons tapioca flour

2 eggs

 4 - 6 carrots (1 1/2 cups grated)

1/4 cup coconut oil

1/2 cup unsweetened applesauce

1/4 cup sweetener*

1 teaspoon baking soda

1 teaspoon baking powder

1 tablespoon ground cinnamon

1 teaspoon vanilla

1/2 teaspoon sea salt

Cashew Cream Filling

1 cup cashews

2 - 4 tablespoons sweetener**

1 teaspoon cinnamon

1 1/2 cups water

INSTRUCTIONS

1. *Soak cashews in 1 1/2 cups water overnight. Drain and rinse.

2. Preheat oven to 350 degrees F. Line muffin pan with paper liners or coconut oil.
3. Grate or chop carrot in food processor or bullet blender until coarsely ground. Add to medium mixing bowl with eggs, oil, applesauce and sweetener and beat with hand mixer or whisk.
4. Sift in almond flour, baking soda, baking powder, spices and salt. Mix to combine.
5. Use ice cream scoop or tablespoon to scoop batter into muffin tins 1/2 - 2/3 full.
6. Bake 15 - 18 minutes until muffins are golden brown and tops are firm to the touch.
7. Remove muffins from oven and let cool about 10 minutes.
8. For *Cashew Cream*, process soaked cashews, sweetener and cinnamon in food processor or bullet blender. Add water 1 tablespoon at a time if necessary, just to smooth.
9. Cut hole in top of muffin about 1 inch deep and spoon in *Cashew Cream*. Or fill pastry bag fitted with 1/2 inch tip with Cashew Cream, and inject muffin with cream.
10. Serve warm or room temperature.

**stevia, raw honey or agave nectar

Sausage Stuffed "Corn" Muffin

Prep Time: 10 minutes

Cook Time: 20 minutes

Servings: 12

INGREDIENTS

1 cup almond flour

2 eggs

1/4 cup coconut oil

2 tablespoons unsweetened applesauce

1 teaspoon sweetener*

1 teaspoon apple cider vinegar

1 teaspoon baking powder

1/2 teaspoon ground turmeric

1/2 teaspoon ground white pepper (optional)

Filling

8 oz ground natural sausage (or sausage patties)

2 teaspoons ground sage

INSTRUCTIONS

1. Preheat oven to 350 degrees F. Line muffin pan with paper liners or lightly coat with coconut oil. Heat small skillet over medium-high heat.
2. Add sausage and sage to skillet and sauté about 5 - 8 minutes, until cooked through. Break up sausage if in patties.

3. Beat eggs in medium mixing bowl with hand mixer or whisk until thick and slightly foamy. Add oil, applesauce, sweetener and vinegar. Mix well.
4. Stir in almond meal, baking powder, turmeric and pepper until combined.
5. Use ice cream scoop or tablespoon to scoop batter into muffin tins, about 1/4 - 1/3 full. Spoon sausage over batter. Then top with second scoop of batter. Fill each muffin cup only 1/2 - 2/3 full.
6. Bake 15 - 18 minutes until edges are golden brown and tops are firm.
7. Serve warm. Or allow to cool and serve room temperature.

stevia, raw honey or agave nectar

Baby BLT

Prep Time: 15 minutes

Cook Time: 25 minutes

Servings: 4

INGREDIENTS

Sandwich Bread

1 cup tapioca flour/starch

1/4 - 1/3 cup coconut flour

1 egg

1/2 cup warm water

1/4 cup coconut oil

1/4 cup applesauce

1 teaspoon apple cider vinegar

1/2 teaspoon baking soda

1/2 teaspoon sea salt

Bacon Dressing

Bacon drippings

1/4 cup coconut oil

2 tablespoons organic mustard

Filling

8 strips nitrate-free bacon

1 tomato

4 romaine lettuce leaves

INSTRUCTIONS

1. Preheat oven to 350 degrees F. Line sheet pan with parchment paper or coat with coconut oil.
2. In medium bowl, sift together tapioca flour, 1/4 cup coconut flour, baking soda and salt. Stir in warm water and oil.
3. Whisk egg in small bowl. Add applesauce and vinegar. Then add egg mixture to flour mixture and mix until well combined. Add 1 tablespoon coconut flour or water at a time if needed to form soft and slightly sticky dough.
4. Divide dough into 4 portions and roll into round or oval balls. Dust your hand with extra tapioca flour to prevent sticking.
5. Place rolls on sheet pan and pat down slightly. Bake 20 - 25minutes, or until edges are golden brown and the tops are firm. Remove from oven and allow to cool.
6. While *Sandwich Bread* is baking, heat large skillet over medium-high heat. Cut bacon strips in half and add to hot pan. Cook bacon until crisp and cooked through. Set aside.
7. For *Bacon Dressing*, add excess bacon grease to food processor or bullet blender with coconut oil and mustard. Blend until light and emulsified.
8. Slice tomatoes. Rinse and dry lettuce, then chop. Slice cooled *Sandwich Bread* in half and spread on *Bacon Dressing*. Layer a few slices of bacon, tomatoes and lettuce pieces on bread.
9. Serve immediately. Or wrap in plastic wrap or parchment and store in lidded container.

Cheese Steak Sandwich

Prep Time: 15 minutes*

Cook Time: 25 minutes

Servings: 4

INGREDIENTS

Sandwich Bread

1 cup tapioca flour/starch

1/4 - 1/3 cup coconut flour

1 egg

1/2 cup warm water

1/4 cup coconut oil

1/4 cup applesauce

1 teaspoon apple cider vinegar

1/2 teaspoon baking soda

1 teaspoon sea salt

Almond Cheese

1 cup skinless almonds*

2 tablespoons coconut oil (or walnut oil)

1 tablespoons lemon juice

1 tablespoon apple cider vinegar

1 garlic clove

1/4 teaspoon ground white pepper (or black pepper)

1/2 teaspoon sea salt

1/4 cup water

Filling

8 oz beef steak

1 small onion

1/2 bell pepper

1/2 teaspoon ground black pepper

1/2 teaspoon Sea salt

INSTRUCTIONS

1. *Soak almonds in enough water to cover overnight. Drain and rinse.
2. Preheat oven to 350 degrees F. Line sheet pan with parchment paper or coat with coconut oil.
3. In medium bowl, sift together tapioca flour, 1/4 cup coconut flour, baking soda and salt. Stir in warm water and oil.
4. Whisk egg in small bowl. Add applesauce and vinegar. Add egg mixture to flour mixture and mix until well combined. Add 1 tablespoon coconut flour or water at a time if needed to form soft and slightly sticky dough.
5. Divide dough into 3 portions and roll into loaves. Dust your hand with extra tapioca flour to prevent sticking.
6. Place loaves on sheet pan and pat down slightly. Bake 20 - 25 minutes, or until edges are golden brown and the tops are firm. Remove from oven and allow to cool.
7. While *Sandwich Bread* is baking, add all *Almond Cheese* ingredients to food processor or bullet blender and process until smooth. Add 1 tablespoon of water at a time to reach preferred consistency.

8. Heat medium skillet over medium-high heat. Add 1 tablespoon coconut oil to hot pan.
9. Thinly slice steak, onion and pepper. Add steak to hot pan and sauté about 1 minute. Add veggies, salt and pepper. Sauté about 5 minutes, until meat is cooked and veggies are soft and caramelized. Remove from heat and set aside.
10. Slice cooled *Sandwich Bread* in half and spread on *Almond Cheese*. Layer meat and veggies on bread.
11. Serve immediately. Or wrap in plastic wrap or parchment and store in lidded container.

Printed in Great Britain
by Amazon